Crown of Violets

Words and Images Inspired by Aphrodite

Temple of Aphrodite Asteria
Laurelei Black, editor

© 2010, Asteria Books
Martinville, IN

Crown of Violets

Words and Images Inspired by Aphrodite

Project Editor: Laurelei Black
Cover Art: Clinton Moore II

This book is a devotional offering to Aphrodite made by each of its individual contributors through the Temple of Aphrodite Asteria.

To learn more about the Temple of Aphrodite Asteria, visit www.templeofaphrodite.org.

Black, Laurelei ed.
Crown of Violets: Words and Art Inspired by Aphrodite.
ISBN 1451522304
EAN-13 9781451522303

Keywords
1. Aphrodite 2. Hellenismos 3. Hellenic polytheism 4. Devotional

Contents

Marble statue of Aphrodite, found headless at Baiai in Southern Italy. The head, neck and right arm have been restored by the Italian sculptor A. Canova (1757-1822). 2nd c. CE. *National Archaeological Museum of Athens, Greece.* Photo by Harita Meenee

Offerings to Aphrodite
By Sophie Reicher

I give to You, Aphrodite --
Urania, who blesses those who fit
nowhere else.
I give to You, Lady,
the hot rushing flood of pleasure,
terrifying, unexpected, secretly sweet.
I give to You the swell of desire,
wetting the aching crevasse
between my thighs,
the body's pounding need
to be mastered and owned.
I give to You, oh Mistress of pain and pleasure both,
the tremble his gaze evokes,
when he turns those predator's eyes upon me
sensing, I think, all untold, my weakness.
I give to You, merciful One,
the hunger his scent draws forth,
the silent need to feast my hands and eyes
upon his bronzed and hairy flesh,
the sharp crackle of skin upon skin,
even if my hands' obsession is only sated within the most
secret recesses of my mind.
Desire
Lust
Hunger
Love
And all the confusion they bring.
Because I do not understand these things,
I will entrust them into Your care,
that they not be tarnished
by my own endless terror
and fumbling attempts at peace.

These things I give to You
that I may learn to celebrate Your gifts
fully even in the embrace of my fear.
Let my fear make them all the sweeter.
I give You these things, Splendor,
that I may return them one day
(perhaps) to him whose hands and sun kissed hair, and comely legs
torment my dreams
Sanctified.
Sacer
Made holy by fire;
because it is the best I can bring
to lay upon Your altar,
that I may learn to embody these hungers well.
In the brutal hegemony of my survival,
Your gifts I've often neglected
denigrated
ignored.
I was too good for them
or so I thought
never realizing
I was diminished
without.
Forgive me, Lady,
and do not hold my foolish pride,
the twistings of my fearful, ignorant heart
against me.
Hail Aphrodite,
called Urania,
succor of the broken,
I bring You these gifts.

Enter My Temple
by Laurelei Black

Enter My temple
And be subdued by the glittering flame
In golden braziers.
Be enveloped by the flaming incense that
Rises from My altar.

Intone My name –
Kypris, Kytherea ... Aphrodite –
And feel My subtle touch
In your most intimate places.

My priestess beckons you
With her cleansing waters
And her healing touch.
My waters.
My touch.

She dances the swaying and undulating
Rhythm of Love's ancient round.
Each movement is practiced and perfect
But fresh
And new
And all for you.

Wrap yourself in beauty
And walk in love
On polished stones of ancient foundation.

You need Me,
And I am calling.
Waiting.
Know Me once more.

"Aphrodite's Bath" by Laurelei Black, © 2008, acrylic on canvas

Aphrodite Soteira
By Melia Suez

Told by a friend to a friend about a friend...
A long time ago, in a time far away
A merchant made a fortunate find
in the last port before homeward bound.
Archaic in style and only a span high
A statuette of Aphrodite,
Patroness of Naukratis, his home town.

Carefully wrapped in rugs
tied securely to the main mast
the holds being too full
with bounty from other ports.
The ship set sail
the crew joyously heading home.

Near Egypt, the sky started to storm
the seas started to pitch and boil.
Was it Zeus and Poseidon trading blows?
Or did the sailors forget their offerings?
It matters not, all that matters is the now.
The ship was rocked and tossed,
It was sent up and it was sent down.
It was waved from side to side.
The motion of the ship was so violent
that even the hardiest sailor became sick.

Huddled near the main mast,
Both merchant and crew found themselves
Sick, miserable and afraid.
Visible was the statue
The rugs inexplicably gone.
Oh Aphrodite Euploia, Oh Aphrodite Pontia

Save us from the water depths.
We are your children from Naukratis
Oh Aphrodite Eiplimenia
Deliver us safely home!

Before their very eyes,
the ropes became green myrtle
scenting the air so sweetly
that their stomachs became calm
as did the raging sea and sky.
As the sun warmed their skin
their spirits did rise
for to home, to loved ones
they would return!

As soon as the ship came to rest
in their beloved home port
reverently the Merchant rushed
the savior image and myrtle boughs
to her temple near the docks.
There he gave offerings of thanks
for a safe home coming,
dedicating the statuette to the temple.

A feast of thanksgiving he then threw
for friends, family and crew
in the temple of Aphrodite
Giving out garlands of the sweet myrtle
That adorned the ship
Calling them Naukratite
And praising Aphrodite's name.

Dance
By Laria

Golden waves lap at
The shore of my soul;
They dance under your
Smiling influence;
I dance for you, too,
My golden mistress,
My laughing lady—
And, if you ask me,
I will never stop.

Photo © J.C. Raley

Not a Bimbo
by Laurelei Black

Ignorant
Rash

Jealous

You don't know Her

Prom queen
Cheerleader
Beauty pageant poser
Airhead

You've taken the façade
the false beauty
and imposed
your narrow
misconceptions
onto the Lady of Love

Beauty is not vain
though it knows itself

Love is not malicious
even when it
rages in desperation
and makes madmen
or corpses

Beauty is the food
of artists, poets and philosophers

Love is the force of creation
the soul's first song
and its last

Golden Queen
Initiator in the sacred rites

This is Aphrodite

Ode to Aphrodite
by Sappho, translated by Harita Meenee

Come here as in past times,
hearing from afar my cry,
you paid heed and left your father's palace,
yoking your gold chariot

you arrived; lovely swift
sparrows brought you on dark earth
flapping hard their wings
from sky through ether.

Instantly they came; and you, a smile
on your immortal face, oh blessed goddess,
you asked what I have suffered
once more, why I called

you and what my frenzied heart
most wants to happen. "Who again do you
long for? Who should Persuasion bring to your love?
Who wrongs you, Sappho?

Because if she avoids you, soon she'll pursue you,
if she doesn't accept your gifts, she'll offer hers,
if she doesn't love you, soon she will
though she may not want to."

Come to me once more and free
me from painful thoughts,
what my soul desires, fulfill
and become, yourself, my ally.

A contemporary statue honoring Sappho. Perched on it are two doves, sacred birds to Aphrodite. Mytilene, Lesbos. Photo by Harita Meenee.

Aphrodite's Gifts
By Melia Suez

Your gift to man is love.
Not only Romantic love,
but also between kin.
There is maternal and paternal love,
love of nature,
love born of friendship,
love of one's fellow man,
love of pets,
love of one's homeland,
and love of self.

Your gift to man is beauty.
Beauty is in the eye of the beholder.
It is subjective and can be found
in the exotic and in the mundane.
It can be found with laughter
and with tears.
It can be internal or external.
Beauty can build one up or
tear one down.

Your gift to man is strife.
Strife born of jealousy,
strife born of desire,
from envy that turns one green
to despair all covered in black,
to chaotic lustful impulses.
You upset the status quo
to force man to grow.

Your gift to man is sex.
Sex with a loved one,

sex with a stranger,
whether done alone
or within a group,
painful or kinky or vanilla,
with male or female partners.

Your gift to man is anger.
Anger born of righteousness,
anger born of indignation,
from vision clearing
to seeing nothing but red
as it shows a depth of feeling.

Your gifts to man are many.
They bring pleasure,
they bring pain,
they let us know we are alive.

Golden Lady, Heavenly One, Mother of All
I hail thee, lovely Aphrodite.
I thank thee for thy gifts.

"Birth of Aphrodite" digital image © 2008, Natalie Long

Evocation
By Melia Suez

Love is a spell that I use
To evoke thee, oh Aphrodite.
Every time I say the word,
I'm calling to thee,
For you are love in all its many forms.
Sometimes it is to ask thy protection.
Sometimes it is in anger or despair.
Whatever the emotion behind the call,
Know that I honor thee, oh Golden One,
And wish for thy guidance and blessing.

Devotee's Prayer
By Laurelei Black

Aphrodite, hear my cry!
Laughter-loving – Philommedes,
Acidalia – from Your bath,
Violet-crowned Kytherea,
I call You by these names and any others
That please You!
Come to me from the shores of Paphos on Cypress,
From your cliff-side caves,
Or from any place where You abide.
I am Your devoted one,
Your servant, Your lover.
You know me by my deeds –
By the songs I have sung in Your honor.
You know me by the blessings You have given me –
The great loves and joys and pleasures of my life.
Come to me again
And bless me
With Your presence.
Allow me the moment's grace
To be near
Love.
Touch me
And receive my touch.
This union of what is Divine in me
With all of Your Divinity.
I offer you the sacred flowers
Of my heart
And my passion
As gifts unto You,
Most adored Aphrodite!

Hymn to Aphrodite
By Lykos

Aphrodite, oh fair one of Olympos,
Your beauty defies words,
The love and passion of hearts is yours.
Goddess, thief of man's heart,
White-armed seductress, your gifts are potent.
Praised be your likeness and your powers.
I worship you for your appearance but more
For your gifts and your message, sexuality.
Please, keep the passion, burning bright,
Alive between my lover and I.
As we move forward to marriage,
May your presence be near and
May we always be true.
Blessed are you of Kytherea!

"Scarlet Woman" by Laurelei Black, © 2009, acrylic on canvas

Scarlet Woman
By Laurelei Black

I wear the red with pride
for I am no plain matron.

When I take you into my
sacred
bedchamber
you will know that I am
Aphrodite's daughter,
Ishtar's pupil,
a woman of the light.

Let me lay you down
among the crimson and golden cushions
below the grape-colored canopy of
my bower.

Lie among the rose petals as
I enter your heart
and hold you in the eternal embrace
of the beloved.

You will never leave me.
Our shared touch will
remain on your skin.
You will share me
with your lovers,
and I will visit your dreams.

I am your Muse,
your Sappho,
your Helen,
your Elissa.

Love me
and find bliss.

Painting © Lykeia

Ecstasy
By Laria

Moonlit ecstasy runs through me.
I look to the sky; I hold my hands out,
Seeking to touch that which I cannot—
Seeking you, my goddess: Aphrodite.

The passion-stirred night-creatures
Sing amongst themselves; rabbits lie,
Together, in shady glens, with silver light
Trickling down over their dark fur.

The nymphai of the cities dance,
Heeding your night-call, O Kythereia.
They pick up slivers of broken glass
And trail them over sleeping humans' flesh.

As all gods and humans know, it is you
Who most controls the body and spirit.
It is you to whom I yield, for you that
Love rushes through me, burning the shadows away.

To Hephaestus
By Laurelei Black

The iron weight of your
measured silence and step
might crush me,
though I've put my golden
suppleness intentionally
in your sights.

You owe me no tenderness,
no obligatory care.
I will not ensnare you.

... but ...

How I long to hold you,
enfold you, caress you,
entice you, excite you, inspire you.
Oh, how I desire you!

The smallest touch is bliss,
but I am of the Ocean and
I want more.

Your light and fire and heat
to meet
my rush and flow and wave.

The lava and the sea foam –
Life's Elixir –
for us to share.

Alchemy
By Laurelei Black

Tvbal Qayn
Tu'Bal Cain
Vul'can

Mighty man of fire
and alchemy.
Bender, shaper, tansmuter
of hardened steel
and supple gold.

Towering, hard,
sweaty, sooty, calloused,
bruised, burned and burnished.

Feared and outcast,
your gifts have two-edges.
Sword, plough, golden sash.

Her passion for you,
Her cooling quench –
These are Mysteries most won't see.
How can Fire and Water love?

Beautiful Boy
By Laurelei Black

Beautiful boy.

No, you aren't quite a man,
but neither are you the child
whose mother is gone
leaving you womanless in the world.

Ha!
YOU without a woman?
That *other* has her claim on you
and you don't deny her –
Spring's maiden
and Death's reigning Queen.

But I see your love
and desire
for me.
Though you may also love
another,
your desire
and affection
for me has never failed.

Radiant youth,
we reflect each other's light
and I am enraptured
by your embrace.

Hold me again
beneath the myrtle tree
where your story began
and where it
must end.

Amor Vincit Omnia
By Laurelei Black

You sweep me away,
A bird of prey claiming the tender prize.
Off my feet and into your arms
Then into my bower
And the golden net
Of passion,
Of love.

My warrior brings hard battle
And conquest
Into every land.
But by me you are subdued.
The hardened ram ridden
By the dove.

The Gift
By Melia Suez

"Give me something..."
"Oh! I got this golden crown on my last..."
"No. Something you've made."
He looks at his hands.
Callused from weapons use.
Scarred from taking hits in the course of his duties.
The same duties that she once had long ago.
Things were different for him then.
He may have been able to carve something crude
But not now. He has lost the knowhow.
He's lost the ability.
Certainly nothing to compare with her beauty.
Or with the gifts from the Master Craftsman
That decorate her bower, her person.
It is just one more thing he can't give her,
Can't be for her.
He looks up at her.
One large solitary tear rolls out of his eye.
Concerned, she reaches up to wipe it away.
As she touches the tear, it solidifies
and settles into her palm.
Eyes wide, she cradles it.
"It is beautiful."

Shrine photo © Lykeia

Anchises' Sonnet
By Laurelei Black

I'm not too much. I'm just a girl, my love.
No Goddess lurks behind my touch or glance.
Don't fear the joy that we have both dreamt of.
Don't turn away and start that lonely dance.

It can't be true. I've seen your grace and shine.
No mortal woman makes me feel this way.
And so the heartache all the more is mine,
Having touched you, if you go away.

But from our love will spring the greatest things.
Our passion's pure, so let me hold you close.
I do not seek to be the sire of kings,
Yet can't resist those sweet green eyes of yours.

My heart and arms will keep this fond embrace.
My soul will ease in welcome of your grace.

Digital image by Anu-Liisa Varis

Aphrodite
By Lykeia

Dripping in pearls, like drops of foam
You have risen from the roaring sea
Coiled with roses, musky perfume, blood red
Entwined, you have risen from your lover's bed.
The dawn is breaking, the night does flee
There you rise, like a naiad, from your bath
The sparkling drops running down your breasts
To pink blossoms drifting on the currents,
Teary pearls making a path one after the last
To drifting petals about your ankles and thighs
And you rise, Aphrodite, brilliant star of the sea
And you rise, heavenly gem of the west and east
Hail, Cypris, with blooming fingers and
Swaying dance you entice with limpid eyes
Hail to you, fairest Dionaea!

Not Beautiful
By Laurelei Black

I may be her daughter,
but I am not the Kyprian remade.
No golden sash compels
my lovers.
Nor could it.

What beauty I have
is a faint reflection of Hers.
Very faint.

Sincere praise of a false impression,
paid to me,
once.
Twice. More.
Heartfelt, but undeserved.

She shines –
golden, pulsing, brilliant –
through a plain vessel
and illuminates it.
Fleetingly.

It is her mark upon me.
Her anointing.
Wiped clean away
when she leaves.

"Aphrodite and Eros" by Laurelei Black, © 2008, pencil on paper

Pen and ink © Lykeia

Hymn to Aphrodite and Eros
By Lykos

Goddess, you of quick-glances and white arms,
You of honeyed voice and perfumed hair,
You of enticing form and beckoning finger.
Praise to you lady of lusting love
And of fiery passion in the marital bed,
And also, oh Goddess, in the extramarital bed!
I worship your beauty and welcome you
In times when my passion must be unbridled.
You of least humble appearance,
Did marry he of most humble form,
I praise you for this!
Blessed is the bliss of your delights,
Praised be you and your name oh Aphrodite!
God, you of the golden arrow and gilded bow,
You of blind choice and stinging dart,
You of welcome countenance and charm.
Praise be to you young son of Aphrodite,
Of the love that rings true through years,
And praise be to you God of lustful love!
I worship your gifts and welcome you
Into my heart when I am filled
With thoughts of my lover.
Blessed is your bow and what it brings
And may your darts never be leaden,
Praised be you and your name oh Eros!

Picking Apples
By Laria

The boughs of the tree are weighed gently down
By apples, gleaming gold in the morning light.
Mists, trembling, unfurl over the earth, as Eos rises
To warm the human world with her shimmering heat.

You pluck one of those apples, when the dawn fades
And the sky begins to turn summers-day-blue.
You hold it to your lips and breathe in the scent;
You stand wreathed in Helios' light, golden, gleaming.

Your body, Kypris, is a mystery known to few; it is your nature,
And your domain, that so many are aware of. For it is you
Who brings love, borne of your body, time and time again –
You bring it to a mother's eyes and lovers' eager lips.

Clarity and dizzy murkiness fall equally beneath your sway,
For you, queen of the human body, are mistress of all of their
Mysteries; it is through your will that the Theoi are honoured
For all begins with you, and it is you alone who can end every-
thing.

Devotion to Aphrodite
By Lisa Marie McDevitt

Oh Aphrodite, Goddess of love and beauty, killer of men....

I thought you were the killer of me.

I did not understand, refused to see
What you wanted me to Learn

But you would not give up
You refused to be ignored

And I am eternally grateful for that,
Shining Goddess.

You are not to be trifled with
You are not a beautiful doll
Filled with nothing but dust

You are vital, You are Woman
You are Power

You are Sex, and everything
That Sex brings with it.

There is no fear
There is no shame

There is Desire, and Attraction
And Joy

Aphrodite, Fair and Heavenly

Thank you for your time, your persistence

Even your anger

Hear my Song

And know of my Respect and Admiration

Hail Aphrodite

The Bountiful, The Merciful, Golden, and Black of Night

You let no one underestimate you.

Of War
By Laurelei Black

Keep "fluffy"
and "sweet"
and take off the
rosy glasses

Battle Goddess
Avenger of crimes
against Love

Passion drive us into hell
to face the gore
the slaughter

Love pushes us in

If not to keep love
to avenge it

Love of place
of home
of wife or child
of friend
of ideals and values and all that is
intangible
and touches us

Love defends
all in its domain
with scratching, biting,
ripping,
gnawing,
grinding
beating need.

War is her mate
and passion is their bond.

Digital image © Sky Samuelle

Epitymbria
By Laurelei Black

Woman of the tombs,
Dark dove of night and death,
You are the perfection of beautiful decay,
Of exquisite grief.
Bereft of Your lover,
The love you shared
Lingers
Like a ghost
To haunt You.
A vision of light and warmth
That gives no comfort.
Your graceful feet
Are sooty with the dust of the Dead
And their places of repose.
Hollow eyes and cheeks.
Hollow heart.
You hunger for the fruit that has rotted
And is beyond Your lips.
Lady of Mourning
And Sorrow
And Loss,
Bleed your darkness onto the cairn,
Onto the pyre,
And wait
For the hope
Of renewal.

Her Vengeance
By Laurelei Black

Irritate Her
at your peril.

Insult Her
far from me.

Wrap yourself in a cloak
of self-importance and
vanity
and think yourself more lovely
than Love.

I dare you.

I've read the warnings,
seen the harvest
of jealousy's reaping.

I want none of those plagues
upon my head.

She turns no cheeks
nor is She gentle, meek or timid

If you value your grace
good-looks
romance
or peace
Give Her honor and thanks
for the blessings She
bestows.

Invocation of Aphrodite
By Belenus

On Wednesday, January 27th, 2010, during the hour of Venus with the moon in Cancer and growing full, I invoked Aphrodite once again. With a red candle burning and offerings of rose incense and wine, I respectfully asked Aphrodite to bless me and you, my readers, with a special Valentine's Day message. I asked her how we could bring more love and beauty into our lives and for anything else we might need to know at this time.

Although I did not see her image or hear her voice this time, she gave me many thoughts in response to my queries, and I scribbled them down as soon as I heard them. I have transcribed here, word for word, what she told me:

"Nature abhors a vacuum. Empty yourself in my name and I will fill your cup with love and bring beauty into your awareness. Have faith; if you are reading this, you are no doubt on the right path. Your star is rising.

Be of service and you will receive more than what is asked of you. Again, I say, empty yourself, and I will bless you. Be of good cheer, cooperate, and do not give into hate. Meet anger and hate with the light of love. Act in my name, the name of love, and I will give you the strength you need.

What you are after, give to others. If you want glamour, recognize and acknowledge glamour in your friends and family. Give away enthusiastically what you want for yourself. If you want friendships, be a good friend to others. Build people up and focus on the good in them and in the world."

I meditated immediately on her words and pictured many of these things happening for me. I asked for her help in emptying myself of ego, for this is never easy for me, and she responded to this request as well. I felt peace and I knew it came from a power greater than myself. I thanked Aphrodite for coming to me and I once again pledged my love and devotion to her.

Aphrodite is the most beautiful of the gods. She is strong, can be demanding, and often not for the faint of heart, but she loves beyond imagination and the world would not have beauty without her divine presence. Thank you. It is always a pleasure to bring you these stories. I'll be back again in March with something new.

Contributors

Anu-Liisa Varis is a graphic designer residing in Finland.

Belenus teaches at the Grey School of Wizardry (www.greyschool.com) and is the founder of Dreamz-Work Productions (www.dreamz-work.com), through which he publishes.

Clinton Moore II is a priest of Pan and the cover artist for this devotional anthology.

Harita Meenee is a Greek independent scholar of classical studies and women's history. She has presented cultural TV programs and has lectured at universities in Greece and the US. She is the author of four books, as well as of numerous articles published in Greek, British and American magazines. She has translated W.K.C. Guthrie's *Orpheus and Greek Religion*; her English translations of ancient and modern Greek poetry have been included in various anthologies and journals. She has a special connection to the Goddess of Love, about whom she has written the book *On the Path of Aphrodite* (in Greek). Website: www.hmeenee.com

J.C. Raley is 45 years old and has spent most of his life in Oregon and North Carolina. He has studied and followed several paths over the past thirty years, with Henry Thoreau and Aleister Crowley as his unlikely pair of guiding stars.

Laria is a polytheist, primarily Hellenic, and has been for about half a year at the time of this publication. The god

she honors most is Aphrodite, and she hopes to eventually become a priestess for Her.

Laurelei Black is a contemporary priestess of Aphrodite and the author of *Aphrodite's Priestess* and *Cult of Aphrodite*. She is the founder of the Temple of Aphrodite Asteria. Website: www.aphroditepriestess.com

Lisa Marie McDevitt is a Hellene and makes poetic devotions in honor of The Twelve.

Lykeia is a priestess of Apollon and devotee of Artemis. Most of her devotional activities extend to poetry and painting, both gifts she thanks Apollon for daily as god of inspiration and the light so necessary to the artists eye.

Lykos (aka Adam King) is a young Hellene who seeks to glorify the Gods in everything. He is an avid poet and fiction writer and currently lives in central California.

Melia Suez is an eclectic Hellenic Pagan dedicated to Zeus who discovered writing when she discovered this spiritual path. Her works are a tribute not only to the chosen subject but also to Hermes.

Natalie Long is a Pagan and occultist. She is initiated into British Traditional Wicca and the Ordo Templi Orientis. Natalie helped found the Babalon Rising Pan-Thelemic Festival and the Midwest Women's Goddess Retreat. She considers herself both a Witch and a Hellenic Reconstructionist. Natalie lives in Central Indiana with her two consorts. In all things she praises Athena.

Sky Samuelle is a college student and aspiring Medical Doctor. She is a solitary polytheistic Witch with an obsessive interest in Celtic and Greek mythology. She lives in Italy, and she loves cooking and the whole gothic sub-culture.

Sophie Reicher lives in NYC where she is a student of language and of history. A devout Pagan, she is currently working on her first book of verse.

Also Available from Asteria

Non-Fiction

Aphrodite's Priestess — Laurelei Black
The priestesshood of Aphrodite is not dead or dormant. It is alive, vibrant, passionate, and growing again. People are stepping forward from places like the US, Belgium, Brazil and elsewhere - stepping forward from the shadows of ancient temple ruins - to construct new practices of worship, celebration and transcendence based on acts of love, beauty and pleasure.

Aphrodite's Priestess (the 2nd edition - revised and expanded - of Laurelei's elegant and ground-breaking work, In Her Service: Reflections from a Priestess of Aphrodite) is the first book to offer readers insight into this re-emerging temple culture.

Cult of Aphrodite: Festivals and Rites of the Golden One — Laurelei Black
As Aphrodite's followers grow in number around the world, Laurelei Black provides them with practical resources to practice the rituals historically associated with the mystery cult of Heavenly Aphrodite. This liturgical compilation offers individuals and groups a solid starting point for honoring Aphrodite.

Fiction

Temple of Love — Laura Britton
She was the ancient world's most famous female poet, writing lyrical verse for the men and women she loved. In this historical fiction offering by Laura Britton, see the life of Sappho through the lens of Aphrodite's priestesshood.

www.asteriabooks.com

Made in the USA
Middletown, DE
23 June 2022